Jeff Altman
The Big Game Hunter

How to Avoid
Being Laid Off, Excessed, RIF'D, Terminated, Axed, Furloughed or Made Redundant:
And What to Do If You Are

You do not have resale rights or giveaway rights to this book. Only people who have purchased this book are allowed to view it. If you believe you have an illegal copy or know someone who does, please email us at TheBigGameHunter@gmail.com The author and publisher of this book and accompanying material have used their best efforts to prepare it. The authors and publishers make no representation or warranties with respect to the accuracy, applicability, fitness, or completeness of this guide. They disclaim any warranties (implied or expressed), merchantability, or fitness for any particular purpose. The authors and publisher shall in no event be held liable for any loss of any damages, including but not limited to special, incidental, consequential, or other damages. The authors and publisher do not warrant the performance, effectiveness, or applicability of any sites listed in this book.

This guide contains material that is protected under International and Federal Copyright Laws and Treaties. Any unauthorized reprint or use is strictly prohibited.

© Jeff Altman, The Big Game Hunter™ Asheville, NC, 2020

Table of Contents

Introduction *1*

What Are Your Reviews Saying? *10*

How to Avoid Getting a Pink Slip *12*

The First Few Stages of The Unemployment Cycle *16*

Before Layoffs Happens *19*

Should I Start Looking or Wait to See If I Can Get a Package? *22*

"Can I See You for a Minute?" *25*

I Wasn't Laid Off . . . This Time *30*

I Don't Have a Job. What Should I Do Today? *33*

Getting Started Again *36*

In Closing *40*

About Jeff Altman, The Big Game Hunter *41*

Previous Books *42*

Introduction

I was part of a men's support team for more than seven years. We called ourselves a team, rather than a group because in teams, you can be cut; in groups, everyone can participate, even if they fail to meet standards.

Once a week for seven years, we met and helped one another with personal and professional issues. We were men with different backgrounds and experiences—a set designer, an entrepreneur, a photographer, a writer, a computer professional, a martial arts instructor and me, the head hunter, all connected from our experiences with one another and committed to supporting one another get what we wanted out of life.

It was pretty common for meetings to become stale so, after a while, we needed to re-evaluate what we did and how we did it. We all agreed to meet a particular weekend to work on this when a day later I discovered that the date we agreed to conflicted with another meeting I wanted to attend in Philadelphia.

I called the others and asked that we change the date to another one.

"But you made a commitment," one said.

"Yes, but it was before I knew it conflicted with this "once a year meeting" that I always attend was a short train ride from New York City where I lived at that time.

"Yes, but, you made a commitment to us and we've all set aside the time to meet!"

We went in circles for a while until I decided that I would go to Philadelphia to attend the meeting and told them that I intended to do so. One man said that there might be dire consequences if I missed the weekend.

When I returned from Philadelphia, there was a message waiting for me on my answering machine.

I had been cut from the team.

I was hurt and furious.

Even though I had received a warning, I never expected to be cut and now had to work through the many feelings that surfaced after I was fired.

The Big Picture

Every few years, things change in business and, with those changes, come layoffs.

Once upon a time, there were two companies—Burroughs and Univac. Then there was one—Unisys. Thousands of jobs disappeared as they did each time a company changed its business focus.

I remember when Japanese automakers started to successfully sell cars in the US and automobile workers in Detroit were laid off in large numbers.

Another time, automation replaced jobs in manufacturing.

Outsourcing to Asia caused companies to layoff knowledge workers.

NAFTA sent jobs to Mexico.

On and on.

Then, there was the sub-prime collapse causing jobs to be eliminated, not just in the financial services community, but across the economy. Then, on top of that, gas prices rose to record prices in 4-6 weeks.

Now, we have a pandemic causing millions to be unemployed and businesses closing.

Businesses and consumers have cut back on spending. The news every night scares people into believing the world is going to end.

It has happened before.

It is happening now.

It will happen again

AND it will probably affect you now or in the future by putting your job in jeopardy.

I have no idea what the trigger will be for layoffs in the future; I just know that layoffs will happen again.

My Story

I was in the job search business for what, at times, seemed like 100 years. As I like to say, "I help the world find work and organizations achieve their objectives by hunting down leaders and their staff."

I wasn't always mature about my work. As a matter of fact, when I started working in the recruiting industry as a 20-year-old college graduate, I was pretty arrogant. I didn't really care about the people I was supposed to help and was more interested in earning a commission, even if it meant doing things that, today as an adult, I am not proud of having done.

I've easily spoken to hundreds of thousands of people at times when they were laid off, fired, or have just decided that the grass looks greener elsewhere.

When I was in my 40's, I thought of making a career change and becoming a psychotherapist in private practice, returning to Fordham University in New York City where I earned an MSW in Social Work (I say I earned an MSW because between working full time in as demanding a profession as mine. I concurrently attended classes and did fieldwork 15 hours a week).

I met my wife, Sharon, in graduate school and put aside thoughts of being a psychotherapist full time but still wanted to look for ways to help people, beyond being a recruiter.

In 2006, I published "Get Yourself Hired NOW!: The Big Game Hunter's Guide to Head Hunting Your Next Job and Every Job After That!" (available in e-book and audio formats) and "Get Your Job Search Organized NOW!" (available in e-book format only). They are available at www.getyourselfhiredNOW.com

This report synthesizes my experience as "The Big Game Hunter", an extremely experienced professional recruiter with my Masters in Social Work (someone who I helped find work for described me as being like a big game hunter and the name stuck).

I am not someone who is writing a book by going to the library, taking five books off the shelf and saying, "Okay how do you do this?" I'm someone who has been on the other end of the phone when a person has called after being laid off!

I'm the person who listens to them grieve their job loss, who takes them by the hand and helped re-construct their psyche so they could perform well on interviews, all the while, serving my corporate clients who are paying me to evaluate, assess, refer (and sometimes reject) people.

I can't say the all the questions here are mine.

Many come from listening to the experiences of people who have been through tough times and helping them get through the hard times so they can show their stuff on interviews and then excel at their next job.

What You Can Expect

Maybe you're expecting a layoff at your company.

Maybe you met with your manager and someone from human resources and were told that you were being laid off.

Maybe your company hired a hatchet man or woman as a consultant who brought you into a conference room and told you that your job was being eliminated (not that you were fired or laid off).

Perhaps your company assembled a group of soon-to-be former employees in an auditorium and broke the news to you.

Maybe you were someone who worked for the firm for ten years or more and believed you had a future with it. Maybe you saw it coming and were racing to find another job when your company beat you to the punch by laying you off.

However it happened, you are out of work or expecting to be out of work soon.

Your partner, wife/husband, parents, friends, children are asking you, "How's it going?" Although you know they mean well, you're starting to become annoyed or may have already bitten someone's head off.

"Survive a Layoff Like a Pro" will help you with your transition from being an employee of your last company and then help you get focused on working on finding your next job. It will give you ideas and a focus so that you can move ahead When you finish this program, you will walk away with a better understanding of what you are going through.

By reading and re-reading this book, you may avoid being laid off and gently transform yourself so that you can look for work without a chip on your shoulder or without the look on your face that says "damaged goods. Instead of hacking through the jungle while you are hurting or feeling particularly frustrated (hurt and frustration that will interfere with you getting your next job), I will help you get into gear to answer the ads, do the networking, make the phone calls and myriad other tasks that will go into finding your next job.

Stay Off The List!

When I was a young boy, my father would take me to Orchard Beach in The Bronx where I would play on the beach and in the water.

Like most fathers, he was concerned about my well-being and would look in the sky for storm clouds and then turn on our portable radio to get a weather report.

If the weather report said that it would be a quick passing rain shower, we would plan on riding things through under a tree. The report indicated thunderstorms, even though the storm might pass quicker than the rain shower, we would leave the beach and start our long trip back. To my father, there was no place to seek shelter that was safe during a thunderstorm.

Keep an Eye on the Weather

If you can't answer the question, "What are the trends in my industry," you are in danger. You are in danger because your ignorance and obliviousness will eventually be punished.

If you have no idea how sales are at your company, what is going on in your field, or how the economy is doing, you might find yourself in trouble because you won't have any idea that the boat is taking on water and might be ready to sink.

There are economic changes that few people can anticipate but there are plenty that can be spotted.

For example, very few people were privy to the calamity that became Enron or the sub-prime industry collapse. Sometimes, people are working with retailers who pretend not to notice that sales are collapsing and that no one is buying things when they walk in their store. They seem oblivious to the fact that people are walking out empty-handed.

Some people seem genuinely surprised to discover that no one is buying the cars their company makes and that the only way they do is with interest rates that are extremely low or with "cash back" at the time of sale.

I remember a time where I was a new graduate working for The City of New York. I wanted to change the world through serving in government but wound up in a mind-deadening job. The people I worked with were more concerned with how long it would be until their next coffee break than in doing their job. As children, they kept trying to cheat the system by arriving 8 minutes late and trying to leave 20 minutes early and not be caught.

The effort was rewarded with ostracism by the staff and attention by the commissioners. I didn't care about their bad manners. I did grow to care that the commissioners would leave every few years and be replaced by a different group of politicians who wouldn't know and might not care because she might have a friend who worked with the agency who would whisper criticism of me in her ears and result in my being fired for because I wasn't friendly with the lazy incumbents.

It didn't seem like a good idea to stay so I left the government and went to work for an employment agency; their effort was the gateway to success and fit my personality and attitudes far better. As was my intention when I went to work in government, I was in a role where I could help people—help people find the kind of work they wanted instead of dying on the vine like an aging tomato on a tomato plant in summer.

I was fortunate and saw the storm clouds gathering on the horizon and realized that, eventually, thunder and lightning would come down and erase me from the landscape. Too often, people keep their heads down, doing their job, getting along with their co-workers, and don't take the time to understand what is going on around them that could affect their job, their career, and their long-term professional success.

What Are Your Reviews Saying?

Most organizations give employees performance reviews to clear the air about where they are satisfied and where you can improve. These are a message from management about how you are seen by them.

PAY ATTENTION!

It can be the first signal you receive about where you stand. Also, they can provide enormous support if your manager leaves or is laid off.

A manager I helped many times found himself in a pickle. His direct manager, a director with the firm, left for another opportunity just in time for the budget cuts to be evaluated and the staff to be cut.

Trying to buy himself some time, he met with his new boss and offered her his previous three performance appraisals as something to consider as she made her recommendations for staff cuts.

What Goes Into a Review?

You are evaluated based upon as many characteristics as there are stars in the sky.

Ultimately, you will be evaluated by whether you exceed, meet, or do not meet certain benchmarks.

These may include quality, timeliness, teamwork, productivity, knowledge of your job, adaptability, dependability, initiative, resourcefulness, leadership, planning and organizational skills, ability to train/mentor staff, communications ability (both oral or written), attendance, and punctuality, a well as how you maintain internal controls (several of these are for managerial staff).

Think and act like someone who has money invested in your company. Would that person put in half an effort or 120%?

How to Avoid Getting a Pink Slip

Pay Attention to Your Relationship with Your Boss or Manager

Do you respect your boss? Do you "like" him or her?

If you don't, often the feeling is mutual. Since they are often an advisor to who winds up getting fired, who do you think they will recommend? You or the one they like?

Here's a variation on that.

Have you noticed a recent chill in your relationship with your boss?

Often a chill is a signal of a problem. Sometimes, it is a signal of their worry about their job. Whichever it is, it is important to pay attention to such changes. After all, if your boss is laid off, who will be there to attest to the quality of your work?

It is critical to nurture relationships with your manager.
Take part in the office rituals—the birthday parties, the lunches—and be a part of the fabric of the office. Don't be the one that everyone talks about. When they talk about you, it is rarely positive.

If you meet a senior manager on the elevator, use it as an opportunity to "talk up your role.

When they ask, "How's it going," the wrong answer is something like "As well as can be expected," or "OK, I guess."

Be prepared to speak about what you have been doing professionally in 30 seconds or less. Speak of your recent work and your successes.

Do You Generate Revenue or Are You an Expense?

Which one are you-- a moneymaker or a cost? Even if you are ostensibly a cost, do you do things that save the firm money? Does management know that?

A client of mine had a receptionist working for them who was an absolute delight. She was cheerful at any time of the day, polite, professional, and genuinely helpful.

Even though the firm was firing people, Molly kept answering calls and everyone loved her. Even a person who is ostensibly an expense can cause people to notice their contribution to their success.

Even if you are a moneymaker, a bad attitude can make you a target of termination.

After all, who wants to be around a pain in the you know where? Firms will transfer your clients to someone else and get rid of you.

Become Indispensable

If you are hidden away in your cubicle, if you are someone they only see over video or speak to me over the phone, you will miss out on some of the plum assignments. It's important to stay connected with your manager, with the people that you serve in ways beyond simply the work assignment.

Come up for air and volunteer for or invite consideration for the work that management is particularly interested in.

Find a way to connect with people as people.

If you aren't part of a critical project or critical work, see if there are ways where you can become involved.

It's harder to be chosen for laid off if you or someone that everyone knows, likes, trusts, and respects.

Ask Yourself The Question, "Why Should They Keep You?"

Ultimately, this is the question that management will ask itself. How do you rank using different metrics by comparison to others? Is yours a department that can be eliminated with no one missing it or is it critical?

When I was a beginning recruiter, working in my first recession, I grew to see that most businesses had three types of employees:

1. People who did things
2. People who managed those who did things
3. People who thought of how things could be done better

During recessions, almost every person who is a #3 is eliminated. Businesses don't care about how things should be done better (even if they should). They are focused on making more money, reducing their costs, and surviving the storm. Some #2's will be used to both manage and think of ways to do things better. Although #1's and #2's may be cut, #3's are often eliminated.

As such, if you are a #3, see how you can move back to being a #2.

Bad Tactics to Avoid Layoffs: Do Not Use These

A former partner of mine said, "Desperate people do desperate things." These are things not to do.

1. Ask for a meeting with your boss and cry about how you can't afford to lose your job
2. Do not get pregnant to avoid being laid off
3. Do not file a lawsuit just to avoid being laid off
4. Do not request information about the company's policies about sexual harassment or discrimination of any sort just to avoid being laid off (if you are being victimized sue the bum and the firm).
5. Do not make a false claim to obtain disability
6. Do not meet with HR and claim that everyone's out to get you (they will be after the meeting).

Chapter 2

The First Few Stages of The Unemployment Cycle

Stage 1. Before a layoff, your office may start to rumble with rumors. People often start to talk or gossip about what they have heard and what's going to happen next.

The fact is that the staff doesn't know anything and is trying to make sense out of what is a scary situation. No one knows anything and everyone believes something. As a result, everyone talks and a lot of people attempt to interpret different contingencies and speculate about things they hear from one another that may have no basis in reality.

Absenteeism often increases as people become ill or try to get a head start on job hunting. Managers start to approach select employees.

You are not on the list.

It may be true today, but it may not be true in three weeks. Someone I met several years ago was told she was not on "the list" by her boss who missed the meeting where she was added to it.

And he missed the meeting where he was added to it, too.

You are on the list. Getting pre-notice can be helpful. It's like getting told that you can have a head start in a race. You are going to be fired with the next layoff. Start looking now.

A woman I know with a bank has been told by her boss that she is going to be in the next staff cuts. According to bank policy, she knows her severance package already so she is using the time to get her resume ready and go out on interviews.

If you stay until such and such date we have a sweet deal for you,

During the period before an acquisition, a young computer support person I knew at a financial firm was approached to stay on board until the acquisition closed. He did a lot of work for a group that was extremely successful and also did work for a previous Chairman. If he stayed, he was told he would receive double pay until the deal closed and 9 months severance.

There was only one problem.

The acquiring firm wasn't in on the discussions and shrugged their shoulders. The young man was invited to join the new firm and, thus, wasn't entitled to anything in the way of severance.

See what I mean about rumors and private deals?

Stage 2: The Layoff

After the initial shock, there is a feeling that feels almost like relief that occurs.

The ax has fallen.

The waiting is over with and everyone knows where they stand.

After a little while, reality sets in, and relief changes to anger and depression.

As Dr. Margaretha Voss wrote in The American Journal of Public Health in 2004, "Unemployment may cause a deterioration of the economic situation, downgrading of social status, broken social relations, changed risk behaviors, impaired psychological well-being, and depression, consequences that may develop into a severe illness."

You see, now you're home or working from the outplacement office trying to find work. Everyone is asking you, "So, how's it going?" All you want to do is find a job and return to normal. That's because being laid off, fired, "excessed," "RIFd" is socially horrible.

No one is throwing a going away party for you and nothing is lined up for you to do. You are stranded on the island of limbo and need to push against all the thoughts that you have and others have about being laid off.

"One person told me, "As much as I loved taking my kids to school and seeing them more often, I was a fish out of water, not knowing what to do with myself. Then my daughter asked, 'Daddy, why don't you have a job,' and I thought I would die."

Chapter 3

Before Layoffs Happens

When things look bleak, most people stick their heads in the ground as an ostrich does. It explains why so many people allow their homes to go into foreclosure instead of picking up the phone and calling the bank's workout department to make other plans.

I have been blogging about the job market since August 2001. Change is part of the competitive landscape and it is critical to be prepared in advance of being laid off.

Here are three things you can do to be prepared just in case you are laid off.

1. **Develop an emergency fund** If you think that you might be at risk of a layoff and do not have much in the way of savings, it is critical to develop a rainy day fund. Having a rainy day fund allows you to pay your bills while you look for work. It won't give you peace of mind—only having a new job will offer you the possibility of that—but it will give you something valuable—financial staying power. The ability to be out of work looking for a job longer is something you will value because it allows you to wait for a job that meets

your goals, instead of taking any job that is offered. If you do not have savings and are not sure how to develop any for your emergency fund, notify your employer that you want to suspend contributions to your 401K and put aside the money in case you need it.

2. **Develop a new budget** This starts by figuring out what you are spending your money on NOW and noting what your assets are that could be liquidated if you needed to. A financial organizer will help you see what your bills are, what your assets are (both liquid and illiquid), and help you see where your money goes. I don't presume to know your family and what is right but Junior might not need three new pairs of sneakers. You might not need cable tv on all six tv sets or a vacation to Australia this year. Paying attention to your expenses **proactively** allows you to make intelligent decisions before you reach a crisis.

Why is it that when someone loses their job, they feel they need to take a long vacation that they "deserve to take." People run up huge bills with a lengthy trip and come home to debt and no job to pay for it.

Trust me. You don't need a vacation. You need a job. Before you start the new one, take a week off for a trip right before you start.

3. **Apply for credit** As I write this, I have not had a dollar's worth of debt in three years. This doesn't mean I am a miser. I have paid off my home, we travel regularly and we do well. But the time to borrow money is when you don't need it and having a line of credit available to you just in case you need access to cash. But first, before you start running up bills, create a new budget, and stick to it!

In most religious systems, wasting money is a sin and foolish. You may need to incur some debt while you look for a job. You can also need to take on a part-time job delivering pizza or driving a limo. You may need to start a part-time business in your home.

Whatever you do, managing your financial resources **proactively** is essential.

After all, employers can sense when a job candidate is desperate during the interview. Like being on a date with someone who is nervous, a desperate job applicant rarely gets hired and, if they are, it is for less money than they might otherwise deserve.

Part of avoiding the feeling of desperation is managing your money so that you don't feel nervous that you **HAVE TO** get this job.

Chapter 4

Should I Start Looking or Wait to See If I Can Get a Package?

When the rumors start at your company, there are two instincts people have—put their head in the ground or head for the hills. Heading for the hills may be a good choice but staying may also be a good one.

Here are several reasons to wait until you are offered a package:

1. **You expect a large severance package** Many organizations have standard practices for how much they will pay someone in case of layoff. In the olden days, many banks would pay an officer of the bank four weeks salary for every year of service. Someone with 10 years of service would be getting a minimum of 40 weeks of pay. For someone earning $100,000 per year in salary that's more than $75,000. Add accrued sick time, vacation time, and personal time and you could easily be receiving more than $80000 to wait to be laid off

2. **Your job history isn't the best** Your job history was, at best, mediocre when you joined this company and if you wait 6 months, you will have two years of service with them. Even if you are laid off, you will have a

severance package and the ability to say that you understood your previous history was somewhat spotty and was trying to clean it up.

Leonid was someone I knew like this. He had been a consultant for many years and his employer was in trouble. He held on and made two years of service, effectively eliminating the "job hopper question" from his interviews. He was able to say to potential employers, "I had been a consultant on a series of six to nine-month assignments for several years. I joined Magna Corp because I wanted to put down roots and stay with a company for many years. Unfortunately, business conditions changed at Magna. Even when they started to become a source of speculation, I stayed because I wanted to contribute to a turnaround and because I didn't want to jump ship so fast."

3. **You receive additional pension benefits by remaining** If you are fortunate enough to work for a company with a pension plan, look at your benefits plan to see whether there is any additional benefit you receive from your pension for remaining longer. If you have already vested sufficiently for maximum benefit and won't receive any more vesting by remaining with your company any longer, don't use this as a reason to remain with them.

1. **Tuition reimbursement** Stay long enough to complete your course and be reimbursed for tuition
2. **You can receive paid-for-training that will enhance your skills in the job market** If your boss will approve a course that will help you in the job market, take the class.
3. **You will vest in some benefit if you remain a little longer** Providing the company you work for doesn't become the next famous business failure, you may benefit from vesting in your stock options or stock grants. Find out now, rather than wait.
4. **You would need to repay a loan** If you borrowed against your 401K or received some preferred loan that you would need to repay immediately upon your departure, don't leave yet.

I don't know your circumstances. I do know that you need to make conscious choices given all the variables you are presented with.

Chapter 5

"Can I See You for a Minute?"

I have always told people that when a manager is asked, "Can I see you for a minute," on Friday afternoon, they know that the person is about to quit and quickly start to calculate whether or not to seek authorization to make a counteroffer.

When a manager approaches an employee late in the day and asks the same question, often it is the signal that you are about to be laid off.

Most people are shocked when it happens, even when they thought they were mentally prepared for it to happen.

It's like a scene from the Godfather when Clemenza is going to take Michael to a meeting with his rival in the other gang and Michael suddenly pulls away. Clemenza is left surrounded by thugs and the consigliere.

Generally, you will walk into an office where your manager, someone from human resources, and perhaps one or two others are present. Like Clemenza in the movie, you have arrived at your execution with everyone participating.

"As you know, the firm has been experiencing some problems financially and we've decided to layoff several hundred (or several thousand) people."

And with that incantation, you will soon hear that you are among the ones who are going to be fired. Laid off. Participating in a RIF. A reduction in workforce.

Whatever the language is, that is the ultimate outcome. You have been canned.

Sometimes, companies give you 90 days' notice to find a job. Sometimes, you are told that there is no reason for you to stay. They will pay you for the next two weeks. Thank you for your service.

A friend of mine was called into his manager's office, fired, asked for the keys to his company car, put in a car room a car service, and driven home

However, it is told to you, they are telling you that they don't want you anymore.

Severance consists of several elements:

Financial:
1. A cash award, commission, bonus, and deferred compensation due to

    you. Rights under your pension, profit-sharing plan, and 401K.
2. Accrued vacation and sick time payout due
3. Reimbursed business expenses
4. Stock option statement and exercise schedule

Insurance:

1. Health, dental and life insurance, as well as disability insurance
2. Information about COBRA coverage (how long are you eligible to remain on your current insurance plan and at what cost)

Post-Employment Services

1. Are you eligible for outplacement? For how long? What will outplacement offer you
2. References
3. Letters of recommendation
4. Access to your office voice mail (having office voice mail gives people the impression that you are still working for the company and that can improve your bargaining position for a new job

Return of Company Property:

1. Return of the company car, credit cards, keys, mobile phone, laptop, and other equipment
2. Return customer lists and proprietary information

Your post-termination commitments

1. What does your non-compete require of you? Have you signed a non-disclosure (NDA) agreement? How will you be allowed to speak of your work?

2. Are there additional obligations you have under a non-disparagement agreement or confidentiality agreement?
3. **DO NOT SIGN ANYTHING WHILE YOU ARE IN THE MEETING UNTIL YOU HAVE IT REVIEWED BY AN ATTORNEY!**

It is a horrible thing to do but it is not unusual for a piece of paper to be slid in front of you to sign while you are there. You may be told that you won't be paid until the release is signed, all the while people are speaking, making it impossible to concentrate on what you are reading (as though they didn't know that).

Imagine for a moment that you were someone who resigned a year before and was pleaded with to stay with your company and did. Accepting a counteroffer happens with all levels of staff from most junior to the executive suite.

At the senior level, you are probably an older worker where the notion of age discrimination raises the possibility of a lawsuit.

Persistence can often result in an increase in your severance.

Asking for more often results in better deals being constructed for one worker and not another.

As the old saying goings, nothing ventured, nothing gained.

Present yourself differently than the average worker that the employee handbook was constructed for.

After all, you were:

1. A long-tenured employee
2. Someone who took a counteroffer from the company who stayed
3. Someone who was a higher achiever than the average who shouldn't be lumped in with all the others.
4. Someone who needs the termination changed to be on the insurance plan another month

So try to separate yourself from your colleagues who were also laid off and be politely persistent.

You may improve your package and walk away a bigger winner than anyone else.

Oh, yes. Do not tell off your boss.

Chapter 6

I Wasn't Laid Off . . . This Time

The layoffs have occurred and the goodbyes have been said.
You are still at your desk in the same job.
You know it doesn't mean that there won't be another round of layoffs and that you won't be cut then.
I spoke with someone not too long ago who survived four rounds of cuts only to be nailed in the fifth one.
What should you do now?

1. **Do a great job!** Even while you may feel panic, depression, anxiety, and fear as though you were laid off with the others, you achieve little by walking around worrying. Step up to the plate and put in a great effort. Allowing lethargy and depression to take root will only have you interview poorly. Who wants to hire someone who is depressed anyway?
2. **Make sure you have contact information for the departed people** Often the recently departed will be your references. Rather than lose contact with them and scramble to re-connect when you need them, make sure you have phone numbers and personal email addresses for them. Connect with them on Facebook, LinkedIn,

Twitter, or any other website you know they are active on. You may wind up helping them with introductions that can help them find a job and, at the same time, maintain contact with them in case you need them, too.

3. **Make sure your personal files that reside on your office system make it home** If you are caught in the next round of layoffs, you probably won't have time to get these off your hard drive. Do you want to forget your tax records, personal photos and bookmarks, and letters used to prepare your mortgage application in the rush to leave when you are laid off?

4. **Get to the doctor** Although you will be offered COBRA coverage after the layoff, you may not be able to afford it (for individuals, it can easily be more than $500 per month; for families, more than $1000). Get you and your family scheduled to see every relevant doctor and every specialist you can.

5. **Update your resume** The person who gets ahead isn't always the smartest or work the hardest (although those are two great qualities to have). The person who gets ahead is the one who remains alert to opportunity. Sometimes those are internal to an organization; more often those are external. With so many people laid off who will start to land at new firms, don't be caught unprepared if someone recommends you for a new job by not having an up-to-date resume ready. And, now

that you have survived a round of cuts, you know more could be coming so get ready.

6. **Start networking** Start to attend networking meetings. Update your profile on LinkedIn and on the other social network sites to show a professional front (remember to take down the party pictures from these sites and replace them with professional ones. You don't want to lose a job because your online nickname is "The Belchmeister" or "Easy . . . on the Eyes".

7. **Don't turn into a workaholic** I started by saying that you should "do a great job," not "work all day and all night. Maintaining balance will allow you to perform better at work and in your interviews.

Chapter 7

I Don't Have a Job. What Should I Do Today?

When you lose your job, you lose your paycheck. You knew that.

You also lose:

Your benefits

The major activity of your workday life

Your role as a worker and provider

Your self-esteem

Control of your life

Your relationships with your co-workers

As time goes by, most people start to experience a kind of death, like being divorced.

And, it isn't just you who is affected. Your family is, too.

The first time you tell your son or daughter, "Sorry, we can't get that, "or we have to cancel that service the entire family enjoyed, it hurts you and it hurts them, too.

And no one talks about it for fear that someone will become upset.

It's not surprising.

In families that care for one another, everyone tries to take care of one another and they don't want to upset you.

Yet, the fact is that unemployment is associated with increased rates of death, heart attack, alcoholism, and drug use, suicide, homicide, admission to mental institutions, and incarceration.

Am I trying to scare you?
You bet I am!

It's important to understand that if you are fired, laid off, excessed, a part of a RIF (reduction in force), or terminated, your goal is to *survive* a layoff like a pro."

I'm not here to pretend that everything is going to be fine and dandy.

I'm here to help get you through the emotional hell that being out of work can be and help you get focused on getting yourself working on finding your next job. [1]

Try to notice some of the symptoms of stress that may occur and ask your family for their support with it too.

Among the symptoms to be aware of are:

1. Getting sick more often
2. Feeling useless and unwanted
3. Feeling tired all the tie
4. Becoming angry more easily
5. Sadness and depression

6. Eating more or eating less
7. Having more headaches
8. Increased use of alcohol or drugs
9. Being disinterested in everything
10. Feeling bored
11. Having trouble sleeping
12. Can't relax
13. Sexual problems
14. Back and stomach problems

Many of the people I work with are business leaders who have been struggling with some of these symptoms. I sometimes joke with them about staying out of the refrigerator and not watching Netflix every afternoon. I will sometimes yell at them to get going and go network, search the web for job leads, contact old colleagues and use some of the tools I point them to find out who to contact at a firm for a job.

Yet, many of them sit home, bored, complaining about this or that, instead of putting in the effort to find a job.

If you have been seeing a psychotherapist or counselor, it may be tempting to discontinue treatment to save money.

In fact, that impulse is destructive to you and your treatment.

Keep seeing your therapist or counselor, particularly now when you will be going through a challenge, unlike the ones you have faced in the past.

You need the support of a professional during this complicated time. This is not where to cutback now.

Chapter 8

Getting Started Again

I speak with people all the time who are in a funk after they are laid off. They are on the 14th revision to their resume trying to make it "perfect," and haven't been outdoors since they were laid off, fired, "RIF'd," "excessed" . . . whatever word they use to describe it.

Even before you think you are ready to interview, there are things you can be doing to get yourself going:

1. **File for unemployment benefits.** The fact is, you can use the money, and you are entitled to it. Do not let your emotions stand in the way of reason here. Fill out the forms! I remember speaking with someone who was out of work for three months and hadn't filed for benefits yet. When I asked him why he told me he was too busy. I asked, "Gee, for three months you didn't have any spare time to file a claim. Do you know how much money you haven't collected yet?" When I told him, he went there within two days.
2. **If you haven't made a budget yet, do it!** Do not "wing it". Determine your expenses by looking at your last three months' costs. Don't just simply say $3000 on my American Express. What did you spend on your

American Express to make it a $3000 bill? Think for a moment, if I am out of work three months from now, what expenses would I eliminate and do it now! Remember, you are probably going to be paying for your full health insurance costs (if your spouse has access to health insurance, see if you can switch on to their plan). Save your money! Do you need four cars (and their insurance and maintenance)? Every dollar you save now will afford you time as you look for work. HC was someone who was able to last for almost two years despite liquidating his and his family's retirement savings and cutting back dramatically on their spending. No more dinners out, music downloads, expensive sneakers, or lattes from Starbucks. He found his next job . . . eventually. Too often, people make the necessary cuts when their resources are running low instead of before they have put big dents into them. Be an adult and do what is necessary **BEFORE** a crisis occurs.

3. **What are your financial assets** How liquid are they? A terrific painting isn't particularly liquid but a mutual fund is. Speak with your financial advisor before doing anything! I can't stress this enough. Get help here to ensure that you organize any liquidation of assets well, taking into account tax consequences. While speaking with, ask for advice about approaching your lenders,

particularly your mortgage lender, about seeking reduced payments.

4. **Don't become a hermit. Get support.** As I mentioned in the last chapter, if you are in therapy, continue to be in therapy. Hire a career coach to work with you and help you with your focus. I coach people throughout a job search or a career change. There other capable coaches available on LinkedIn.

5. **Schedule a meeting with the outplacement service your company contracted with to help you.** Find out what resources are available to you from them. They will probably prepare the resume for you, provide you access to coaching (not all of which is good) that can help you get going again.

6. **Avoid using your credit cards** Take them out of your wallet or purse and resist the urge to use them. You may find yourself in a store and reach for one to charge something and laugh when you realize it is at home. Good! Better not to add to your debt or wind up in debt by charging dinner, sneakers, or something else that you will forget about in two weeks.

7. **Start talking to people** More jobs are filled by networking than any other manner and you never know when the job lead will turn up from. John Sampson from MIS Networks told me a wonderful story about the man who found a job because of his cleaning woman. It

seems that she kept asking for a resume and he never gave it to her. Finally, his wife demanded that he give it to the woman to shut her up. It seems that the woman's husband was a director with a large firm that wanted to hire someone and Mr. Stuck-Up filled the bill.

8. **Prepare your elevator speech** An elevator speech is aptly named. It is a short presentation, one that lasts no more than 15-20 seconds (as long as it might take to travel from the lobby to the top floor of a building). It can be given at networking meetings, casual events (the kids' soccer game, for example), job fairs, cold calls to employers when you leave voice mail, and any other situation where the subject allows you to give yourself a "commercial." It can also be given by your spouse for situations that he or she finds themselves in, too. There are a lot of "cute" versions of an elevator pitch but, for now, think of extending yourself beyond the words, "I'm an engineer looking for a job," or I'm an attorney looking for a firm to join where I can sue people."

9. **Start contacting recruiters** There may be people who you have used to hire staff at your last job or the one before that. You may get referrals from people you know of people who they think are extremely good. However, you come to them, start contacting recruiters.

In Closing

A layoff is often a difficult experience emotionally because we have so much invested in our work and in our job that being laid off, fired, "RIF'd", "excessed" . . . whatever term it is . . . feels like a failure, even when it isn't one. Well-meaning people keep asking "How's it going?" and offer useless advice and opinions.

Yet, once we realize that, as they say in the Godfather movies, "It's business. It isn't personal," we can start to go out and start working on making this set back into a triumph.

Some of you may take a step back in your career. Some of you will make a huge leap. Others will find that they moved on a lateral plane. Whatever describes you, what is most important is to recognize that your experience is normal and that this, too, will pass.

Thank you to my wife, Sharon Lovich, and my son, Jack Altman, for making the sacrifices and being so supportive, allowing me to spend the time to work on this.

And, thank you to the many millions of you whose resumes I've read and spoken with over my career who have been my true teachers for this program

About Jeff Altman, The Big Game Hunter

Jeff Altman, The Big Game Hunter is a coach who worked as a recruiter for what seems like one hundred years. His work involves career coaching, all as well as executive job search coaching, job coaching, and interview coaching. He is the host of "No BS Job Search Advice Radio," the #1 podcast in iTunes for job search with more episodes than any other show by more than 2:1, a top-rated YouTube channel at JobSearchTV.com plus an OTT television channel available through the Job Search TV app for Amazon and Roku, as well as through BingeNetworks.tv for AppleTV and 90+ smart tv platforms. He is also a member of The Forbes Coaches Council.

If you are interested in 1:1 coaching, interview coaching, advice about networking more effectively, how to negotiate your offer, or leadership coaching? Schedule a free discovery call or coaching session at The Big Game Hunter.us
If you have a quick question for me, you can get it answered with a 3-5 minute video at
www.TheBigGameHunter.us/videoanswer.
Want to do speak with me live? Book 15 minutes at www.TheBigGameHunter.us/live

Connect with me on LinkedIn
at www.linkedin.com/in/TheBigGameHunter

Previous Books

"The Ultimate Job Interview Framework" In paperback and for Kindle

"Diagnosing Your Job Search Problems" for Kindle. Receive free Kindle versions of "No BS Resume Advice" and "Interview Preparation."

"Get Ready for the Job Jungle" Available for Kindle

"Great Answers to Behavioral Interview Questions" for Kindle

www.ingramcontent.com/pod-product-compliance
Lightning Source LLC
Chambersburg PA
CBHW070900220526
45466CB00005B/2066